100% OUR LIVING PLANET

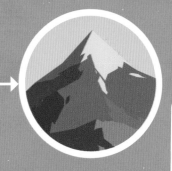

First published in Great Britain
in 2020 by Wayland
Copyright © Hodder and Stoughton, 2020
All rights reserved

Series editor: Elise Short
Produced by Tall Tree Ltd
Editor: Lara Murphy
Designer: Jonathan Vipond

HB ISBN: 978 1 5263 0849 8
PB ISBN: 978 1 5263 0850 4

Wayland
An imprint of Hachette Children's Group
Part of Hodder and Stoughton
Carmelite House
50 Victoria Embankment
London EC4Y 0DZ

An Hachette UK Company
www.hachette.co.uk
www.hachettechildrens.co.uk

Printed and bound in Dubai

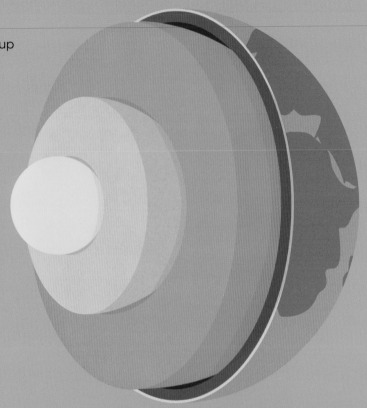

MIX
Paper from
responsible sources
FSC® C104740

FSC
www.fsc.org

Picture Credits
Shutterstock: 1tr, 4rb Romolo Tavani, 1br astudio, 3tc, 12-13
MicroOne, 5br Fotos593, 6-7 ixpert, 6tl Zeljko Radojko, 6bl
Irina Voloshina, 8c Merkushev Vasiliy, 9cl Ivan Smuk, 10tr
WhiteDragon, 10-11 ianmitchinson, 10b, 17tl Designua, 11t
Elena11, 12bl Webspark, 13br Bos11, 14-15t DEmax, 14-15b
trgrowth, 15tr Naypong Studio, 16-17 corbac40, 16b phive,
18tl Armin Rose, 18b Vectors Bang, 18-19 astudio, 21r Sergey
Gordienko, 24tl totajla, 24bl EhayDy, 20-21t Harvepino,
20-21b udaix, 22tr Sentavio, 22bl Dirk M. de Boer, 22br
quangmooo, 23cl Kraipet Sritong, 23br, 31br alexworks, 25br
Shutterstock, 26-27 Vixit, 27tr Roop_Dey, 28l aphotostory,
28-29 ventdusud, 29tl grynold, 29tc Maksimilian, 29tr
leungchopan

Living planet

Earth is the third planet from the Sun in our solar system. It is the perfect distance away to create conditions for life to exist.

Goldilocks Zone

Earth is in a 'Goldilocks Zone', where the temperature is neither too hot nor too cold. If Earth was closer to the Sun – like Venus, where temperatures can reach 462 °C – it would be too hot for life.

If Earth was further away – like Mars, where the temperature drops to -125 °C – it would be too cold.

If a climate is too hot or too cold for liquid water, life cannot exist.

Sun

Mercury
58 million km

Venus
108 million km

Earth
150 million km

Mars
228 million km

Jupiter
778 million km

Saturn
1,427 million km

Uranus
2,871 million km

Neptune
4,498 million km

Sun power

The Sun is what makes our planet support life.

- Its energy heats water that makes clouds, which deliver rainwater
- Winds are created as Sun-warmed air rises and cooler air moves to take its place
- Plants grow using the Sun's energy; the plants then provide food for animals.

Plants need light, water and oxygen to grow.

Layers of heat

Our planet is made up of four layers:

1%
CRUST

The hottest weather on Earth is near the equator. The further north or south you travel from the equator, the cooler the climate gets.

56.7 °C
HIGHEST AIR TEMPERATURE RECORDED ON EARTH, AT DEATH VALLEY IN THE USA

The lowest air temperature ever recorded was -94.7 °C, in Antarctica.

Mantle
Semi-molten rock, around 2,900 km thick

84%
LOWER AND UPPER MANTLE

Core
Earth has a solid inner core and liquid outer core.

Earth's crust
Made of igneous, metamorphic and sedimentary rock, and up to 50 km thick.

15%
INNER CORE AND OUTER CORE

Heat from the core

Currents of heat from the Earth's super hot core spread outward towards the surface. Sometimes this heat bursts out as lava, forming volcanoes.

A volcano erupts, throwing out lava.

The atmosphere

The atmosphere is the layer of life-giving gases around Planet Earth. The gases are thickest close to the surface. Higher up, they are more thinly spread.

Earth's atmosphere

The amounts of the main gases in the atmosphere have stayed roughly the same for around 200 million years:

Living and breathing

21%
OXYGEN

Oxygen

All animals use oxygen to turn food into energy, as well as for building new cells. This process produces carbon dioxide, which is then breathed out.

0.03%
CARBON DIOXIDE

Carbon dioxide

Plants take in carbon dioxide, which is made up of one carbon atom and two oxygen atoms. The plants remove the carbon and use it to make food. They release the oxygen.

30%
INCREASE IN THE AMOUNT OF CARBON DIOXIDE IN THE ATMOSPHERE SINCE THE INDUSTRIAL REVOLUTION

Greenhouse gases

Carbon dioxide, methane, nitrous oxide and other gases form a layer high above the Earth's surface. They trap heat in Earth's atmosphere, but increased levels have contributed to global warming.

0.8 °C
THE TEMPERATURE THE EARTH HAS RISEN BY SINCE 1880. THIS PROCESS IS CALLED GLOBAL WARMING

Nitrogen

Nitrogen is needed by all plants and animals. In the atmosphere, gaseous nitrogen can't be used by living things. Bacteria, lightning and industrial processes can convert nitrogen into a usable form. Earth's usable nitrogen is found in the soil, plants and animals.

78%
NITROGEN

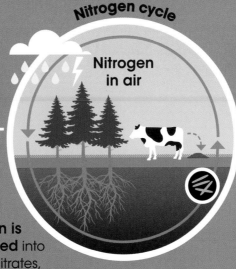

Nitrogen cycle

Nitrogen in air

Bacteria convert nitrates back into gaseous nitrogen.

Nitrogen is converted into usable nitrates, which are used by plants and animals.

Plant and animal waste decomposes, releasing nitrates back into the soil.

0.9%
ARGON

0.07%
OTHER GASES

41,419 m

HOW FAR UP AMERICAN ALAN EUSTACE WAS IN 2014, BEFORE FREE-FALLING TO EARTH FROM A HOT AIR BALLOON

It was the highest skydive ever made, and Eustace reached speeds of 1,322 kph. At just 8,000 metres above **sea level**, there is not enough oxygen for humans to survive. So he had to wear a breathing apparatus and pressure suit.

Water

After air to breathe, the next most important thing for life on Earth is water. You can survive weeks without food (though it wouldn't be fun), but only days without water.

Water cycle

Water is always on the move. Without the water cycle, plants and living things, humans included, would die out.

Vapour rises

The Sun's heat causes water to evaporate from the sea as water vapour. (The salt is left behind.)

Clouds form

The evaporated water cools and forms clouds.

Rain falls

Water collects to form streams, rivers and lakes which eventually flow back to the sea.

Melting ice

Each summer, the ice in glaciers and at the poles melts slightly. It reforms during winter.

Since 1979, the polar ice has got smaller by about 12.5 per cent every ten years. Scientists link this to global warming (see page 6–7).

With less water locked into the ice, sea levels are slowly rising.

1%
OF FRESH WATER IS AVAILABLE THROUGH THE WATER CYCLE

1,630,000 km²

HOW MUCH LESS SEA ICE THERE WAS IN 2018, COMPARED TO THE 1981-2010 AVERAGE

This is the same as having lost a chunk of sea ice nearly as large as the whole of Mexico.

Staying hydrated

Amazingly, only 3.5 per cent of the water on Earth is fresh water. The other 96.5 per cent is salt water, which we cannot drink to stay alive.

Deadly salt water

For humans, drinking salt water can be deadly. You have to pee so much to get rid of the extra salt, you release more fluid than you drink. This causes dehydration.

69%
OF FRESH WATER IS STORED IN POLAR ICE AND GLACIERS

30%
OF FRESH WATER IS LOCKED AWAY DEEP IN THE EARTH

Oceans

Scientists think that life on Earth began in the seas. Today, about half of the oxygen humans and other animals breathe is produced by tiny plant organisms called **phytoplankton** floating at the surface of the ocean.

Phytoplankton

Four Oceans

Geographers divide Earth's ocean into four parts:

- Pacific Ocean
- Atlantic Ocean
- Indian Ocean
- Arctic Ocean.

Smaller bodies of water are usually called seas, gulfs or bays.

71%
OF THE PLANET'S SURFACE IS COVERED IN OCEAN

Pacific Ocean

Atlantic Ocean

Indian Ocean

Arctic Ocean

Rising oceans

Today, global warming is causing sea levels to rise (see page 8). Melted water from sea ice and glaciers is joining the oceans, and warming up. As warmer water takes up more space, water levels rise and can flood low-lying areas.

8.25 cm
AVERAGE AMOUNT SEA LEVELS AROUND THE WORLD ROSE BETWEEN 1993 AND 2018

Seawater

Seawater is roughly 3.5% salt; it also contains traces of every single chemical element found on the planet.

Weather drivers

The oceans drive our weather:

- Evaporation produces clouds, as part of the water cycle (see page 8), which bring fresh water to land
- Winds flow across the ocean from warm to cold areas, or towards the land
- Oceans are where the most violent storms and hurricanes are born.

29%
OF THE PLANET'S SURFACE IS LAND

Temperature control

Oceans also regulate the world's temperature by absorbing the Sun's heat. Currents carry cold or warm water around the planet.

8,000,000 tonnes
OF PLASTIC WASTE IS RELEASED INTO THE OCEANS EACH YEAR

It is eaten by fish and seabirds, who think it is food.

Plastic breaks down into microplastics, containing harmful chemicals. These are absorbed by sea creatures and make their way into the food chain.

Earth's heat

Beneath the Earth's rocky crust are thick layers of unimaginably hot molten rock. The heat comes from a chemical reaction at the Earth's core.

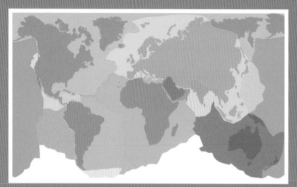

Plate boundaries

Tectonic plates

The heat at Earth's core swirls slowly around, creating convection currents in the rock. These currents move the tectonic plates of solid rock that make up the Earth's crust (see page 14–16).

Heat radiation

Heat from the core radiates all the way to Earth's surface. Very close to the surface (anywhere from 3 to 100 metres down) the ground is usually about 13°C. Right at the surface, the ground temperature is controlled by the local climate.

6,000 °C
TEMPERATURE AT THE EARTH'S INNER CORE

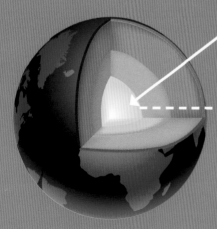

Heat radiates outwards

Earth's inner core
This is the hottest part of the planet. Closer to the surface, the temperatures are lower – but still hot enough to melt rock.

40%
OF KNOWN
VOLCANOES ARE
ACTIVE

Volcanoes

Sometimes the hot molten rock beneath the Earth's crust breaks through – this is what forms volcanoes.

Usually this happens at a place where tectonic plates meet.

Sometimes, a 'hot spot volcano' forms through a hole below a tectonic plate.

1,250 °C

THE TEMPERATURE LAVA CAN REACH

Of the approximately 600 active volcanoes on land, about 10 per cent erupt each year.

At any one time, about 20 volcanoes are erupting somewhere in the world.

There are thought to be almost three times as many volcanoes deep beneath the ocean as on land.

Lava erupts from an active volcano

Dormant volcano

60%
ARE DORMANT
(CURRENTLY
INACTIVE)

Earthquakes

Earth's surface is covered in slowly moving tectonic plates. Sometimes plates become stuck against each other. Tension builds, then suddenly releases – causing an earthquake.

Plate boundaries

Areas that are prone to earthquakes are likely to be situated along fault lines – where the tectonic plates meet.

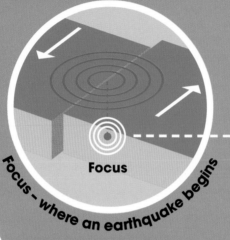

Focus

Focus – where an earthquake begins

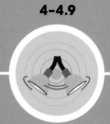

1,370
THE NUMBER OF EARTHQUAKES ESTIMATED TO HAPPEN EACH DAY

Micro-earthquakes

Micro-earthquakes are caused by small tectonic movements. They are not serious and cannot even be felt by humans.

Roughly 500,000 earthquakes happen a year without a single person being disturbed by them.

The Richter scale

Earthquakes are measured on the Richter magnitude scale:

1

2–2.9

3–3.9

4–4.9

1 Micro: Not felt and rarely recorded.

2 and 3 Minor: May be felt, but rarely cause damage.

4 Light: Usually felt, may cause minor damage (objects may fall off shelves).

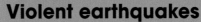

80%
OF EARTHQUAKES AREN'T FELT BY HUMANS AND CAN ONLY BE DETECTED BY MACHINES

Violent earthquakes

About 100 earthquakes a year (0.02 per cent of the total number) cause serious damage. The effects of these earthquakes may be felt very far away.

In 1981, water sloshed out of the University of Arizona swimming pool because of the Michoacán earthquake – which happened 2,000 km away, in Mexico.

Earthquake destruction

ONLY
20%
OF EARTHQUAKES CAN BE FELT BY HUMANS

×31 INCREASE IN THE AMOUNT OF ENERGY AN EARTHQUAKE CONTAINS PER NUMBER ON THE RICHTER SCALE

So a magnitude 2 earthquake releases 31 times more energy than a magnitude 1 earthquake.

5–5.9

6–6.9

7–7.9

8–8.9

5 Moderate: Felt by everyone, may damage weak buildings.

6 Strong: Felt over 100 km away and damages some stronger buildings.

7 Major: Felt 250+ km away and damages most buildings.

8+ Great: Damage to most or all buildings; near-total destruction.

Tsunamis

Tsunamis are waves caused by undersea earthquakes or landslides. In deep water, a tsunami can pass by without you noticing – but when tsunamis reach the shore, they can be deadly.

1. Tsunamis are born

When a disturbance causes the seabed to suddenly drop or lift, the water above it moves too. Then gravity pulls the water back into position.

IN THE OCEAN, A TSUNAMI IS **5%** AS BIG AS WHEN IT COMES ASHORE

Ripples form

Surface wave moves away

Seabed disturbance

Seabed

Ripple effect

2. Tsunamis spread

After the water above the disturbance moves, the water next to it moves too. A ripple spreads out, like the ripple from dropping a stone into a pond.

Pacific ocean

800+ kph

SPEED A TSUNAMI CAN TRAVEL IN DEEP WATER

A tsunami can cross an entire ocean in a day.

About 80 per cent of tsunamis happen within the 'Ring of Fire' in the Pacific Ocean.

3. Arriving at shore

When a tsunami reaches shallow water, it slows down. By now, it may only be travelling at 40 kph.

The wave's trough often reaches shore first. About 5 minutes later, the wave itself arrives.

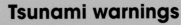

Tsunami warnings

Most tsunamis happen in the Pacific Ocean.

Several countries in the region have set up tsunami warning systems. If the systems detect earthquakes and sudden movements in the ocean, warnings will sound in coastal areas.

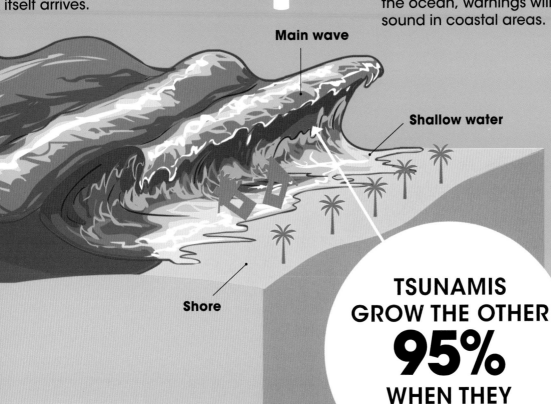

Main wave

Shallow water

Shore

TSUNAMIS GROW THE OTHER 95% WHEN THEY REACH SHORE

Deserts

Deserts are dry areas where few plants can grow. At the moment they make up roughly a third of the land on Earth – but the deserts are spreading.

Antarctica

Sahara Desert, Africa

Biggest deserts

Deserts are not always hot: the world's largest desert is the frozen continent of Antarctica.

The biggest hot desert is the Sahara in Africa. It is over 9,000,000 km², and growing all the time.

249 mm
OR LESS
PRECIPITATION FALLS IN A DESERT EACH YEAR

IF 250–499 MM OF RAIN FALLS, THE LAND IS OFTEN CALLED A SEMI-DESERT

IF LESS THAN 50 MM FALLS, IT MAY BE NAMED A HYPER-ARID DESERT

Spread of deserts

In many places, global warming has led to higher temperatures and less rainfall. This lack of rain is the main reason why the deserts are spreading.

In Africa and Asia, there is a high risk of food growing land becoming desert.

66%
OF AFRICA'S FOOD GROWING LAND MAY BE SWALLOWED UP BY THE SAHARA DESERT BY 2025

Halting the deserts

In Africa and Asia, the spread of deserts could spell disaster – but the authorities are fighting back:

- In Africa, a 'Great Green Wall' of trees is planned to halt the spread of the Sahara

- In China, the South–North Water Transfer will transport water over a thousand kilometres from the south to the dry north.

Great Green Wall

Sahara Desert, Africa

270,000,000
THE ESTIMATED INCREASE IN AFRICA'S POPULATION FROM 2014–2025, YET FOOD GROWING LAND IS SHRINKING

34%
OF AFRICA'S FOOD GROWING LAND WOULD REMAIN, BUT IS THREATENED BY CLIMATE CHANGE

The Gobi Desert in Central Asia is one of the coldest deserts on Earth. In winter, it can reach a bone-chilling -40 °C.

Even in the hottest deserts, temperatures can drop to 0 °C at night. This is because there are no clouds to keep the heat in.

Hurricanes, cyclones and typhoons

Hurricanes, cyclones and typhoons are all the same thing: powerful, damaging storms. People have different names for this type of storm depending on where they live.

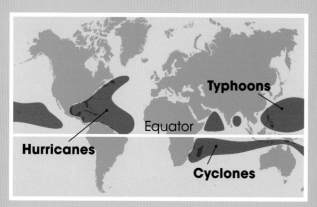

Typhoons

Equator

Hurricanes

Cyclones

44%
OF THE MOST POWERFUL RECORDED HURRICANE SEASONS HAPPENED WITHIN 100 YEARS, BETWEEN 1890–1989

Where to find them:

Hurricane: Atlantic and Northeast Pacific

Typhoon: Northwest Pacific

Cyclone: South Pacific and Indian Ocean

Storm birth

These storms get their energy from warm ocean water.

Because global warming is making our oceans warmer, powerful storms are becoming more common.

Saffir–Simpson scale

There are 5 levels of storm, each one more powerful than the last ...

Level 1: 119–153 kph (wind speed)
Light damage to some buildings and plants.

Level 2: 154–177 kph
Significant damage to some buildings and trees.

408 kph

HIGHEST RECORDED WIND SPEED OF CYCLONE OLIVIA IN 1996

The eye (centre) of the storm is usually calm with no clouds. A giant 'wall' of violent winds and rain rotates around this point.

In the southern hemisphere, storms rotate in a clockwise direction, but in the northern hemisphere, storms rotate in an anti-clockwise direction.

Eye

Tropical storm

56%
HAPPENED WITHIN JUST 28 YEARS, BETWEEN 1990–2018

Hurricane names

Hurricanes make such a big impression that they are given names. The names are taken in turn from six permanent lists, each used for a year at a time.

Sometimes a storm is so deadly that its name cannot be used again, so it is replaced with a new one. This was the case for Hurricane Katrina in 2005.

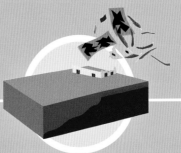

Level 3: 178–208 kph
Buildings and trees sustain major damage, power supplies likely to be disrupted.

Level 4: 209–251 kph
Catastrophic, long-lasting damage to buildings, trees and utilities.

Level 5: 252+ kph
Catastrophic damage, possibly leaving areas uninhabitable for many months.

Forests

Just under a third of Earth's land is covered in forests. They provide habitats for plants and animals, as well as wood for humans to use.

What forests do

Forests are vital for life:

- They provide homes for many living organisms (half of all the world's species live in tropical forests)
- Forest trees and plants take in carbon dioxide and release oxygen
- They store carbon in their structures, reducing the build-up of carbon dioxide in the atmosphere.

There are three main types of forest:

Boreal
Evergreen, coniferous forests found south of the Arctic.

Temperate
Found in cooler regions, mostly north of the equator.

Tropical
Found in warm, wet regions close to the equator.

Forest loss

The amount of land covered by forest is getting smaller.

- In 1990, the planet's land was 31.6% forest
- By 2016, that had shrunk to 30.7%.

The main reasons for forest loss are logging and clearing forests for farming.

Tropical home

Logging

12,000,000 km²

AMOUNT OF BOREAL FOREST IN RUSSIA

Russia's forests are the largest in any country.

They make up 55 per cent of the world's total coniferous forests.

Equator

50%
CARBON

Wood is made of:

6%
HYDROGEN

Demand for products

Forests are often cleared to make space for crops and animal pastures.

Forests are sometimes cut down in one country because of the demands of people elsewhere.

In 2013, for example, experts worked out that Europe's hunger for wood, meat and agricultural products was responsible for about 30 per cent of world deforestation.

42%
OXYGEN

2%
OTHER CHEMICAL ELEMENTS

Wildfires

Wildfires, which are also called bushfires, are fires that spread through dry vegetation. They usually happen in warm places during summer.

Seasonal hazards

When the weather is hottest, vegetation dries out. With no moisture inside it, vegetation, such as grass, can easily catch fire.

88%
OF WILDFIRES ARE STARTED BY HUMANS

12%
HAVE NATURAL CAUSES

1. Hot air rises

Fire causes

Wildfires are caused by:
- Human activity, such as dropped cigarettes or campfires
- Volcanic activity
- Sparks from rockfalls.

Hidden underground

Some wildfires burn underground. Rotting material buried below the surface, such as peat, catches fire. These fires can burn for months, occasionally breaking out to the surface.

100,000

WILDFIRES ON AVERAGE IN THE US EVERY YEAR. THESE CLEAR 16,000–20,000 KM² OF LAND.

Feeding the fire

Once a fire has started it may develop a 'fire front' – a line of flames that moves forward (see below).

- Hot air rises from the fire front, pulling in cooler air from ahead
- The cooler, fresh air feeds oxygen to the fire
- Super-heated trees ahead of the fire release flammable gases, which burst into flame.

2. Flammable gases are released

23 kph

SPEED AT WHICH WILDFIRES CAN SPREAD

3. Cooler air pulled in from ahead

New life

Wildfires are destructive, but they have been happening for millions of years. In some places, the fires even help plant life regenerate.

Mountains

Mountains are landforms that rise steeply above the surrounding land. Mountainous regions cover 24 per cent of the world's land.

Mount Everest, Nepal

24%

600 m

Rocky peaks

A mountain's height is a measurement of how far its peak is above sea level. Most peaks over 600 metres tall are called mountains.

Formation

The tallest mountains form where the Earth's tectonic plates push against each other. The plates crunch up like the bonnets of crashed cars.

The Himalaya Mountains were formed like this about 55 million years ago.

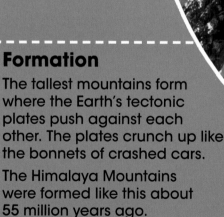

Mountains pushed up

Two plates collide

Precipitation

When clouds reach mountains, they are forced to rise into cooler air. The clouds' moisture condenses and falls to the ground, causing rain.

Precipitation

Condensing water vapour

Moist, rising air

100%
OF MOUNTAINS OVER 8,000 METRES TALL ARE IN THE HIMALAYAN AND KARAKORAM RANGES

Ganges River, India

Rivers

Many of the world's great rivers start life in mountains. The Himalayas, for example, are the source of the Indus, Ganges, Yangtze, Brahmaputra, Mekong, Irrawaddy and Yellow rivers.

8,848 m

HEIGHT ABOVE SEA LEVEL OF MOUNT EVEREST IN THE HIMALAYAS, THE WORLD'S TALLEST MOUNTAIN

Pangaea

About 299 million years ago (mya), Earth had only one large, flat landmass called Pangaea. This supercontinent had no real mountains and few rivers. The land was mostly desert.

Pangaea started to break up about 200 mya, and its tectonic plates began to shift. Some moved apart, while others pushed together, forming mountain chains.

The Earth 335 mya

Pangaea

Cities

Cities cover less than 1 per cent of the planet's surface – but because they are home to over half of us, cities have a big impact on the life of the planet.

In 2008, for the first time:

50%
OF THE WORLD'S PEOPLE LIVED IN CITIES

50%
LIVED IN THE COUNTRYSIDE

Why cities are growing

People are moving to cities from the countryside. Some are pushed by problems such as drought or war. Some are pulled by opportunities such as new jobs. The total human population is growing: by 2050, forecasts say there will be almost 10 billion people on the planet, compared to 7.7 billion in 2019.

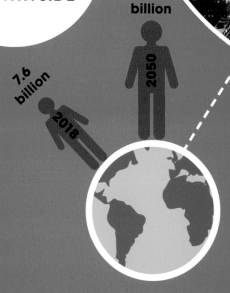

10 billion

7.6 billion

2018

2050

Dangerous pollution

High levels of waste

Using energy

City problems

The growth of cities causes problems for the planet. Most cities create huge amounts of waste and pollution, need lots of energy, and use resources, such as fossil fuels, from all round the world.

37,435,000+

ESTIMATED POPULATION OF TOKYO METROPOLITAN AREA, THE WORLD'S BIGGEST CITY, IN 2019

Vatican City, Rome

Tokyo

The world's smallest city is Vatican City in Rome, with a population of about 800 – just 0.00214 per cent of Tokyo's. Vatican City is also the smallest by area, with just 0.44 km² (about twice the size of Grand Central Station, New York City).

City opportunities

Future cities could help humans have a smaller impact on the living planet. For example, they could become energy-efficient and be designed to produce less waste. Reusing and recycling materials, like plastic, is a good way to do this.

Reducing pollution

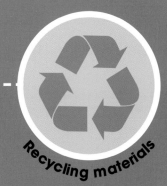

Recycling materials

Glossary

Atmosphere
The layer of gases that surrounds a planet. Earth's atmosphere is made up mainly of nitrogen and some oxygen, with small amounts of other gases.

Atom
The smallest amount of a substance that can take part in a chemical reaction.

Boreal forest
Also called taiga, this is a band of evergreen forest that stretches around the northern parts of Asia, Europe and North America. It is the world's largest biome and to the north of it lies the treeless tundra.

Convection currents
A circular movement of a fluid (liquid or gas), caused by heating one part of it. As the fluid is warmed it becomes less dense and rises. As it rises, it cools, becomes more dense and so sinks again.

Core
The centre of a planet. Earth's core is divided into two parts: an inner and an outer core. The inner core has a radius of about 1,220 km, while the outer core stretches out for another 2,200 km to the mantle.

Crust
The thin rocky outer covering of Earth. Earth's crust is divided into two types: oceanic crust and continental. The crust ranges from about 3 km to 50 km thick and it has been broken up into pieces called tectonic plates.

Equator
An imaginary line around a planet halfway between its two poles and usually around its widest part. Earth's Equator is about 40,075 km long.

Goldilocks zone
The region around a star where conditions are just right for life. Earth orbits in the Goldilocks zone around the Sun and temperatures here are neither too hot nor too cold for liquid water to exist, which is vital for living things.

Greenhouse gases
A collection of gases found in a planet's atmosphere that reduce the amount of heat energy that is lost into space. The main greenhouse gases in Earth's atmosphere are water vapour and carbon dioxide.

Igneous
A type of rock that was so hot that it was liquid, before it cooled and solidified.

Lava
Liquid rock after it has erupted onto Earth's surface through a volcano.

Magma
Liquid rock that is found deep beneath Earth's surface.

Mantle
The layer inside a planet between the crust at the surface and its core. Earth's mantle is divided into two main layers, the upper and lower mantle, and is about 2,900 km thick.

Metamorphic
A type of rock that has been changed by high amounts of heat and pressure.

Pangaea
The huge supercontinent that formed about 299 million years ago and started to break up about 200 million years ago.

Precipitation
When water vapour in the atmosphere condenses and falls to the ground. It comes in the form of rain, snow or hail.

Richter scale
The scale used to measure the strength, or magnitude, of earthquakes.

Ring of Fire
The region lying around the edge of the Pacific Ocean where most of Earth's volcanoes are found. It is formed by the boundaries between several major tectonic plates.

Saffir–Simpson scale
The scale used to measure the intensity of hurricanes.

Sedimentary
The name given to a type of rock that has been formed by sediments deposited by wind, rivers, ice or the sea.

Seismometer
A device used to measure movements in the ground. It can detect earthquakes, volcanic eruptions and powerful explosions.

Tectonic plates
The large rocky plates that Earth's crust is broken up into. These plates are pushed and pulled about by swirling currents in the rocky mantle beneath the crust.

Temperate
The term used to describe the regions that lie between the polar and tropical regions.

Tropical
The term used to describe the regions that lie on either side of the equator.

Trough
In a wave, the trough is the lowest part, as opposed to the crest, which is the highest.

Tsunami
A large, powerful wave that is triggered by an underwater earthquake, eruption or landslide.

FURTHER INFORMATION

Books to read
The Big Countdown: Seven Quintillion, Five Hundred Quadrillion Grains of Sand on Planet Earth
Paul Rockett (Franklin Watts, 2014)
The Big Bang and Beyond
Michael Bright (Wayland, 2016)
Cause, Effect and Chaos! How Things Work On Planet Earth
Paul Mason
(Franklin Watts, 2018)

Places to visit
The Science Museum
Exhibition Road
London
SW7 2DD
The Atmosphere exhibit at the Science Museum shows how Earth's atmosphere works, the ways it is changing and the effects of these changes.

The Natural History Museum
Cromwell Road
London SW7 5BD
The Restless Surface exhibit shows how wind, water and weather have helped shape the Earth. The permanent Volcanoes and Earthquakes exhibit includes information about historical volcanic eruptions, plus modern ways of building an earthquake-resistant house.

HOW TO READ BIG NUMBERS
1,000,000,000,000,000,000,000,000,000,000 = one nonillion
1,000,000,000,000,000,000,000,000,000 = one octillion
1,000,000,000,000,000,000,000,000 = one septillion
1,000,000,000,000,000,000,000 = one sextillion
1,000,000,000,000,000,000 = one quintillion
1,000,000,000,000,000 = one quadrillion
1,000,000,000,000 = one trillion
1,000,000,000 = one billion
1,000,000 = one million
1,000 = one thousand
100 = one hundred
10 = ten
1 = one

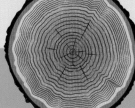

Index